T0079843

Undermining
the Idea of India

THE INDIA LIST

Undermining
the Idea of India

GAUTAM PATEL

LONDON NEW YORK CALCUTTA

Seagull Books, 2022

© Gautam Patel, 2021

The text in this volume is an updated edition of
the Constitution Day lecture delivered online for
The Leaflet, available at: http://www.theleaflet.in.
First published as 'Undermining the Idea of India',
The Leaflet, 27 November 2021.

First published in volume form by Seagull Books, 2022

ISBN 978 1 80309 0 764

British Library Cataloguing-in-Publication Data
A catalogue record for this book is available from
the British Library

Typeset by Seagull Books, Calcutta
Printed and bound by WordsWorth India, New Delhi

CONTENTS

UNDERMINING
THE IDEA OF INDIA

Good evening. It is a privilege to be here, especially today. I must thank Indira Jaising, Anand Grover and their remarkable online journal, *The Leaflet*, for thinking of me for this talk today. From Indira and Anand it was not so much an invitation as a mandamus, but one I gladly obeyed. For I have always held both of them in the highest regard. Over the years, they have been uncompromising and steadfast in their pursuit of justice. In their courage and resilience,

they are the indomitable ones in occu-
pied Gaul. What their magic potion is, I
do not know. But may the sky never fall
on their heads.

❦

Listen to this. India, 2047. 15th of
August 2047. One hundred years since
Independence. A land where the ancient
patterns and rhythms of life are still
unchanged: small, dusty villages, barren
lands, the earth parched and cracked.
Also a land of super-advanced high tech,
artificial intelligence, robots, nanotech.
India is fractured, balkanized into
smaller regional states—Awadh, Bharat
and Bangla. A super-advanced flying
machine, a sort of armed helicopter-
aircraft hybrid, sets down in a dry river
bed. The Ganga has almost entirely dried

up now. There is no water. The states are desperate. Natural water systems are being modified; glaciers forcibly melted. There is even a proposal to tow an iceberg into the Bay of Bengal.

But this is also the centre of the high-tech universe. Artificial intelligences or aeais have personas. The law now bans aeais that imitate humans, ones that pass the Turing test. These are hunted down and destroyed by a dedicated force, the Krishna Cops. But lower-level aeais are everywhere. A long-running television show, or tivi soapi, *Town & Country*, has a cast entirely of aeais. And, on the nightly television news, experts appear on multiple channels, simultaneously, all 'live'.

Clearly, something has gone wrong.

No, this is not the product of my fevered imagination. It is the backdrop of *River of Gods*, a 2004 award-winning science fiction novel by Ian McDonald.[1] I chanced upon it in a small bookshop in Kanpur. I was there on work—I don't imagine anyone goes to Kanpur for pleasure—some strange hearing before a local government satrap in charge of company affairs. The copy I bought from a local bookshop was a large-format paperback, a thick book with a weirdly kitsch cover: a picture of a blue multi-armed goddess and Ganesha, a replica of the kind of posters sold by street vendors.

That book is now nearly twenty years old, but the time it speaks of is not far away, no more than about a quarter century. Some of what it describes is already happening. But the most terrifying part of the book's context is its calm prophecy that India, as we know it today, and as we have known it since 1947, is doomed. It cannot last. It will splinter. States will go to war—over water.

We may dismiss this as nonsensical science fiction, the stuff of overwrought fantasy. But it seems to me to nail down something critical to our conceptualization of who we are, and who our founding fathers meant, or wanted, us to be.

❧

Beyond an arid description of territorial and geographical boundaries, what *is* India? It seems incredible that this enormous land mass, over one-third the size of the United States and of the European Union, with over 17 per cent of the world's population but without a common language, ethos, culture, regional history or practice, should even exist as a single political or national unity.

India is an improbability. By any measure of logic or reason, it should not be. Not in this form.

And yet it does.

And we take its continued existence for granted.

That is a mistake.

India is different things to different people. It is no one thing to everyone. People have very different ideas about what it means to be Indian, and what India is. But there is really only one idea of India, and it is this idea that is the glue which keeps it what it is.

This is the *Constitutional* idea of India.

Even here, people disagree. People speak of the 'idea of India' and link it to the Preamble to our Constitution, or

Part III, the fundamental rights. Discussions and debates seldom go beyond the usual tropes: liberty, freedom, fairness, justice, equality, secularism and so on. Each is crucial. But they are all still components that build on something even more fundamental.

I mentioned a glue. But think instead of an architectural framework or exoskeleton, the outermost structure, something that defines the outer boundaries and limits, gives the structure its shape— in architectural terms, its elevation and its 'built form'. Where do we find this? It is not, I argue, in Part III, though that is the basic structure of the Constitution. If we were to look in the Constitution for the *idea* of India, we should, I believe, find it in an article that is seldom discussed or addressed.

That is Article 1.

India, that is Bharat, it says, *shall be a Union of States*.

Everything in the Constitution flows from this concept—often described as federalism of a particularly subcontinental stripe.

This has to be *the* idea of India; for, without it, India cannot exist. What this incredibly compact sentence, freighted with meaning and implication, tells us is that while we may differ from state to state and region to region, all of us are one. Think of it as a patchwork quilt, colourful, varied, cheerfully disordered, delightfully different, and yet all stitched together.

Consider what happens if we abandon or lose *this* conceptualization, this idea of India.

We find ourselves in the world of Ian McDonald's *River of Gods*.

Within this tapestry or quilt, there are unifying threads that keep it from becoming a set of tattered rags. These are our fundamental rights, and they do not distinguish between the union and its component states. The fundamental rights in Part III of the Constitution hold together this Constitutional notion of India as being a *union* of states.

Article 1 therefore sets the stage for everything that follows. In particular, it leads inexorably to Parts V and VI of the Constitution, again not much in the public eye. These parts deal with the Union and the States, and within each of these parts there is a provision that also uniquely informs this Constitutional idea of India.

The provision is that the governments at both the centre and the state have a limited shelf-life. By governments I mean of course the Lok Sabha or House of the People and the Legislative Assemblies. This means that every five years, the government must seek a mandate for continuance from the electorate.

I believe this concept of time-limited governance is also critical because it necessarily informs our rights; specifically, our fundamental rights. As we shall presently see, these concepts—of governments at both centre and state, of India being a union of states, and of governments having a defined term—are precisely what worry all present dispensations. It is this that every dispensation seeks to conquer or subvert.

Allowing it to happen undermines the idea of India.

☙

It was not always like this. In fact, it was never like this. A broad view of our history shows us something quite different. For millennia, we have had rulers, external and internal. They have controlled and ruled over territories vastly different in size and topography. Some may have recognized regional or local political identities, but these were always in the nature of subservience and fealty to the stronger central power. This concept of self-determination, or of the people choosing who would govern, and of the people being given the right to make that choice, did not exist in our history, at least not on this scale and in this form, until 1947; actually, until 26 November 1949, 72 years ago today, when we formally adopted our Constitution.

The two concepts, therefore, of a Centre–State structure, and of periodic elections of governments at both levels, are a radical departure from anything in the history of the subcontinent. This was, therefore, from the framers of our Constitution, a gigantic leap of faith. It involved putting in the hands of this cacophonous, bickering, amorphous, disparate and non-unified mass of humanity a truly fearsome power, and a freedom of untold and undefinable dimensions: the power of choice, and the freedom to choose by whom we wish to be governed.

Madhav Khosla's *India's Founding Moment*, a book with the delightful subtitle *The Constitution of a Most Surprising Democracy*, speaks of precisely this breakthrough conceptualization by the framers of our Constitution.[2] They knew, he says provocatively, that India's people 'would need to learn the ways of citizenship'—my point precisely when I say that we had no experience of it at all before. But that tutelage was not to be of master and pupil (the colonial British grandly explaining suffrage to the natives). Instead, our framers gave us the whole package. They threw us into the deep end of the pool. They expected us to swim, not sink. And they did this— heaving universal suffrage or franchise at us—in a land of abject poverty, staggering illiteracy, hidebound by the most archaic traditions and socially fissiparous.

Rohit De, assistant professor of history at Yale University, says this in his sharp work, *A People's Constitution*:

> The institution of adult suffrage and institutionalization of the social revolution are the markers of radical change in the Indian

Constitution. The institutional-
ization of universal franchise was
a revolutionary act in a deeply
hierarchical society—especially
when the franchise had only
recently been extended to
women, people of colour, and
working-class men in various
'mature' Western democracies.
Franchise without restrictions
was a sharp break from the very
limited franchise linked to com-
munal identities and property
qualifications that had been pro-
vided through various colonial
reforms.[3]

And yet, somehow, improbably, it has worked. As De says, the Indian Constitution 'profoundly transformed everyday life in the India republic [. . . and] this process was led by some of India's most marginalized citizens rather than by elite politicians and judges'.[4]

The Indian adult populace, one that had never before known that such a thing could be, rapidly cottoned on to the power in its hands. If there is one lesson politicians in post-Independent India have learnt, and learnt the hard way, it is never to take India's electorate for granted. That is also why our elections are so spectacular: India going to the polls is like all of North America and all of Europe going to the polls simultaneously.

So let me ask straightaway: what could conceivably be more terrifying to a politician or their party than the knowledge that their continued political existence is, every so often, in the hands of the great unwashed? As the noise increases—more dissents, more raucousness—so too does the government's anxiety.

I am going to digress slightly here to suggest that it is now time to make a conscious change to our vocabulary. Because of this Constitutional idea of India and this structure, it is time we stopped speaking of 'the ruling party' or 'rulers'. India has no rulers. India is not ruled and so long as the Constitution exists, it never will be. It may be governed—for a limited period of time—but never ruled. The sooner we rid ourselves of this colonial linguistic baggage, the better.

❧

By Constitutional decree, and even otherwise, power is fragile. This in-built fragility, this temporality of power and the risk of interruption, is a threat to every government.

That power to choose a government, and the power to end the term in office of the present government, speaks directly to the concept of choice. That is logically and inextricably connected to the freedoms and liberties we find in Part III of the Constitution. For no one can be expected to make an intelligent electoral decision unless that choice results in an *informed* decision. You cannot have an informed decision, or intelligently make a choice, unless there is a second side to be heard, an alternative narrative, a counterpoint. In other words, a debate; and every debate demands disagreement or a dissenting voice. This necessarily requires the safeguards and guarantees of liberty, and it requires them to be Constitutionally protected. If we invert the paradigm, we see the importance of the linkage: if we merely have the right to decide without the freedom to choose and the freedom to choose without the right to discuss our choices, we are denied the right to act on those freedoms. Then the freedom of choice is an empty promise.

To put it even more bluntly, perhaps in a phrasing no government will like: the right to choose one's own government is an express recognition of the right to disagree with the present government. It is the right to dissent. But it goes further. It is the right to disavow the government and to deny it any legitimacy to continue. And this is not just a right. Because it is tied to universal franchise, the Constitutional ideal *compels* us, every five years, to choose. The right becomes a duty.

Inherent in the breadth and openness of this Constitutional ideal, and the corresponding freedoms and liberties, is an unsettling and uncomfortable unpredictability of result. This is why there are calls, even from within the voting populace, to limit available choices. We should, the argument goes, amend the Constitution so that only those with specified education can stand for elections. No one has yet quite dared to go as far as saying that only the educated or the privileged should be entitled to vote, but I expect the day is not far when that, too, will be propounded.

Successive dispensations seek to circumvent this perceived threat by different means. Dynastic succession, for instance, is an attempt to limit the people's options and curtail the freedom of choice: vote for the father or mother or, if not him or her, the politically reluctant offspring. Other methods are more invidious.

Five strategies in particular have gained currency, and not just here but wherever governments perceive themselves to be under threat. It is equally true, as commentators have said in the recent past, of governments from South America to Eastern Europe, all with claims to being under one form or another of constitutionalism. So these strategies are not peculiar to India, but India is not immune to them either.

The first self-preservation strategy is to criminalize dissent and disagreement altogether. This takes many forms: the deployment of harsh criminal and anti-terror statutes beyond their avowed purpose, and, where it still exists, the invocation of sedition law. The latter has been much criticized. A. G. Noorani, a jurist of exceptional acuity and precision whom I regard as one of our finest legal minds, has written extensively on the subject.[5] More recent are the writings of Dr Abhinav Chandrachud, a very fine lawyer in my court and one who some-how finds the time to straddle the two worlds of a busy practice and studied academic writing.[6] Whether it is in the context of a protest or the cheering of this or that team at a cricket match, their trenchant commentaries argue that the law on sedition is outdated and out of step with fundamental Constitutional concepts of liberty and freedom.

A second approach is to weaponize ordinary laws, such as, for instance, taxation laws. These are openly used as threats to muzzle disagreement and dissent and to ensure that a contrary voice remains unheard. Withstanding or confronting these attempts demands great resilience and, yes, a formidable financial and legal arsenal.

The third tactic is to entirely trivialize the disagreement, opposition or dissent even when it takes a widely visible form. This is actually very effective. The protest often takes the form of a physical disruption of everyday activity—blocking a road or a highway, for instance. When the protesters are portrayed as the lunatic fringe or worse, as causing discomfort to people's daily routines, it is easy to marginalize them and to divert attention from the substance of their disputes.

This endeavour is considerably assisted when those who support the dissenters and protestors manage to get it wrong on facts or on law, or both. A recent example was the consternation expressed about the 2020 Farm Bills by one commentator, a journalist with a stellar track record but evidently with no familiarity with statutes. He wrote a piece critiquing the bills and led with what he considered its most shocking provision—the bar of jurisdiction of civil courts. He wrote that this was an egregious statutory provision peculiar to these bills. As any law student will tell you, it is not, and it has received judicial interpretation for over half a century. It is this kind of wrong-headedness that feeds neatly into the attempts at marginalizing dissent.

The next tactic is to promote an entirely faux nationalism, based on religion or ethnicity, and to warp the concept of nationalism to a purpose never intended by the Constitution. Manan Ahmed Asif, associate professor of history at Columbia University, has a challenging thesis in his recent work, *The Loss of Hindustan.*[7] He argues that the shared political history of the sub-continent is reflected in the works of indigenous historians from about 1000 CE to 1900 CE. That understanding of Hindustan—the idea of Hindustan—he says, was of a multicultural, multi-denominational home. The most complete such idea of Hindustan, he writes, came in the early seventeenth century from Firishta, a historian of Persian origin who served the Deccan sultans. It inspired countless influential European thinkers from Voltaire to Edward Gibbon. Yet, Firishta's notions of a multicultural Hindustan were somehow lost and replaced by a religiously divided subcontinent, one entirely at odds with its own history.

As Romila Thapar has been pointing out recently in her book on dissent and a series of lectures that followed, dissent and disagreement are actually part of our history and historical traditions.[8]

The fifth, and most recent, of these attempts to muzzle dissent is also perhaps the most innovative, and comes from a surprising quarter. A serving bureaucrat said last week that the new frontiers of war, something called fourth-generation warfare, is, unbelievably, civil society. Specifically: civil society can be subverted, can be suborned, can be divided and can be manipulated to hurt the interests of a nation. And he said this to the police, exhorting them to see that 'they', meaning civil society, stand fully protected.

This statement received stinging rebukes from a former IAS officer and a former IPS officer, both of the greatest renown. Each pointed out that their mandate, and their oath, was to safeguard the values of the Constitution. Both decried this attempt to turn the full brunt of the police on the very people the police are meant to serve.

As one of the critics also pointed out, the term 'civil society' was itself unclear. I confess I have no idea what it is supposed to mean, if anything. What is a civil society? As opposed to what? An uncivil society, where everyone is perennially rude? Is this a civil society as opposed to a criminal society? What might that be? The mafia? A criminal society poses no threat but a 'civil' society does? And who is or is not a member of 'civil society'? Journalists? Builders? Handcart pullers? Does it include the police itself? How about bureaucrats? IAS officers? Ministers? And judges? Yes, let's not forget judges. Are they civil society? Are judges a threat to the government?

❧

This is by no means an issue peculiar to India. Surveying autocrats across the globe, Anne Applebaum says this in her superb essay for the December 2021 issue of the *Atlantic*:

> If the 20th century was the story of a slow, uneven struggle, ending with the victory of liberal democracy over other ideologies—communism, fascism, virulent nationalism—the 21st century is, so far, a story of the reverse. [9]

Nor is any of this new. Adam Zamoyski, whose books range from Chopin to Napoleon and Poland, has a spectacularly incisive volume titled *Phantom Terror*.[10] He uses a historical analysis to identify the bases of the paranoia that created modern state policing and generated contemporary societies threatened by subversive forces. I would have liked to quote from this at some length but I do not think time will permit it. So this must suffice:

> In their terror [of the French Revolution, the ruling classes of Europe] saw conspiracy everywhere. Monarchs, aristocrats and politicians—including

Napoleon—set up formidable
police networks to flush out and
destroy the supposed terrorist
cells. But the swarms of spies and
agents provocateurs they mobi-
lized only fed the fear, and led to
the suppression of all dissent and
the persecution of anyone whose
attitude, or even manner of dress,
aroused their wild suspicions.[11]

Ideas are dangerous. And as one popular
graphic novel puts it, ideas are bullet-
proof. So is this Constitutional idea of
India. And that dangerousness, inherent
to the idea, is what takes us to attempts at
censorship and suppression of thought,
expression and dissent. These are, first,

acts of self-preservation by governments, but an intelligent and nimble government will use these to force broad-spectrum illiberalism, especially in culture, art and religion.

Please step back with me to a point at which we began: the Constitutional mandate to vote for or against a government every so often. No government anywhere is comfortable with this; but that is precisely the point. It is a mechanism to keep governments true to their electoral promises. Now if you want to do away with this, and continue in governance, since you cannot do away with the periodic elections mandate, you have to render them useless. That is only done by keeping away all criticism, dissent and discourse and insisting that the government's narrative is the only authentic one. Everything else is criminal, or terrorism, or anti-national and, therefore, illegitimate. But there is always a resistance, and therefore the attempts at marginalizing opposing voices grow. This should be familiar: *Things falls apart. The centre cannot hold. Mere anarchy is loosed upon the world . . . the best lack all conviction, while the worst are full of passionate intensity.* Thus, if there is no legitimate criticism, the reasoning goes, there is nothing to debate or discuss and therefore the electoral result is assured. But this is a progression that the Constitution forbids: a return from the governed to the ruled.

This is a passage I return to again and again. It is from *Kindly Inquisitors* by Jonathan Rauch, a senior fellow of governance studies at the Brookings Institution:

> A liberal society stands on the proposition that we should all take seriously the idea that we might be wrong. This means we must place no one, including our-selves, beyond the reach of criti-cism; it means we that must allow people to err, even where the error offends and upsets, as it often will.[12]

This tells us that dissenters may not be sure of their own positions. But that very uncertainty is what the Constitutional idea of India contemplates. This is the essence of liberty, and we must return today, in 2022, to the words of Judge Learned Hand, one of the three greatest judges from America, who said in 1944 in his *Spirit of Liberty* address, that 'the spirit of liberty is the spirit which is not too sure that it is right'.[13]

So what is the way forward? Is there a way out? Do we have any defences at all? Or is the idea of India—the Constitutional idea of India—doomed, and it is only a matter of time?

I see two beacons. One is familiar and well known and perhaps, from me, predictable. To many, it is the last bastion or the final frontier, depending on your perspective. This is, of course, the judiciary. And it is at its doors that successive governments have always baulked. The judiciary frightens a government seeking to cling to power like nothing else does. Our own history shows repeated attempts to weaken the judiciary, especially during the Emergency. And we are, again, by no means alone: from Turkey to the United States, from Eastern Europe to South America, this is a tale with regional variations.

Has our judiciary withstood attempts to cut it off at its knees? I must leave that for another day. Not because I am fearful of saying what must be said, but because I believe this to be a complex and intricate issue, not easily answered by pointing to this or that individual occurrence. It needs careful and detailed study and measured conclusions. Some other time, perhaps.

But I do insist today that, if we look back across the decades, we find that the judiciary has, in its own sometimes startling way, come through in defence of the idea of India. In 'The Indian Supreme Court and the Art of Democratic Positioning', an essay I believe to be the finest—despite its somewhat lugubrious title—in the compiled volume *Unstable Constitutionalism*, Pratap Bhanu Mehta says this:

> [R]ather, the Supreme Court's behaviour, its exercise of jurisdiction, and the form of arguments it deploys must be viewed in the context of a messy political democracy. It is an institution

that must be mindful of the fact that it is competing with other branches of government for broader public legitimacy and that its exercise of power is an intervention in an ongoing democratic discourse. Therefore, it will not often have the classic rule-of-law characteristics; rather, it will be a messy compromise driven by competing concerns, values and a sense of its own institutional possibilities. The Court's role is more as conflict manager, and its interventions will be tailored to how it perceives it can best manage that conflict.[14]

He goes on to show how the Supreme Court acts as a custodian of what it perceives to be the public interest, and how it is driven by what he describes as an 'inchoate sense of what public opinion requires'. This, he argues at some length, has both potential and pitfalls.

The second bulwark comes from something we take for granted. It is surprising, but its power is very real and truly formidable. Technology; specifically, the internet. For if there is today one thing that obliterates geographical boundaries and makes impossible the kind of censorship territoriality we saw in the 1950s in *Romesh Thappar v. The State of Madras* [15]—a localized Madras ban on a Bombay-based publication—it is the internet. A fundamental truth about the internet is this: no government can shut it down, at least not completely, and not without itself collapsing. Everything the government does, from communication to finance, every single aspect of governance, is now dependent on the internet. Big government and big business depend heavily on online communication. Perhaps they once believed that, like the newspaper barons of the past, they could control it and therefore dictate what went forth and what did not. But it is now nearly impossible to control or choke. Therefore, it does not matter today if someone in America speaks of two, ten, or twenty-nine Indias. Like the smog in our cities, that message will get through, even under the most solidly closed doors. If illiberalism is the biggest threat to a constitutional democracy, then the internet is the biggest threat to illiberalism.

But with it has come, in the last two years, something unprecedented, something unknown in the history of mankind. And something good did come of the SARS-COV-2 virus. I speak of the qualitative leap in access to justice when one marries technology to the justice-delivery system. It is futile to now pretend that online hearings or hybrid hearings are a transitory thing or that we will soon return to our creaky, dusty and expensive ways. It will not happen. More importantly, it should not be allowed to happen. For this, more than anything else in recent memory, has changed the face of the judicial system. So consider what happens when a judiciary with a strong sense of its self offers phone-in-hand access to the highest courts in the land.

This much is clear: the counterpoint and the counternarratives are now, thanks to technology, almost impossible to silence, and they can be heard remotely in courts of law. There may be more adverse comment, and more noisiness now than ever before. But is that not the point? Is that not what our Constitution contemplates, even demands, when it says that the idea of India is embedded in these twin concepts of a union of states and of a Constitutionally mandated choice to give any government its marching orders at defined intervals? In the Constitutional scheme of things, there is simply no such thing as too much noise or too much dissent. If there is one thing the Constitution does *not* contemplate, it is 'the comfort of conformity or the tranquillity of the familiar'.

The seed planted in the Constitution has taken hold. Attempts to uproot it have not succeeded yet. But we should not, I think, be too sanguine. As we have seen, there will be continued attempts by every government everywhere to maintain control—to transition from governor to ruler. That is something we must guard against. To paraphrase something I felt compelled to say in an order, governments will come and governments will go; but the idea of India—the Constitutional idea of India—resilient though it has proved to be, must be protected. And yes, also this: that history will not judge us by our highways or bridges or statues. It will judge us by how well we have preserved the Constitutional idea of India, and saved it from being undermined.

Thank you for listening.

CODA

The day this lecture was delivered, 26 November 2021, the *New Yorker* published a marvellous piece by Adam Gopnik: 'Kurt Gödel's Loophole and Donald Trump's Defiance'.[16]

Gopnik wrote about the 'loophole' that Gödel, the famous logician, is said to have found in the United States Constitution when he was readying himself for a US citizenship test—a way in which a democracy could easily become a dictatorship. The article is beautifully written, and its links worth pursuing. But what

struck me was part of Gopnik's con-
cluding paragraph: that 'the power of
the Constitution is identical with our
commitment to it'.

While this is a compelling thought,
it seems to me to assume that the commitment of individual citizens should
ordinarily be enough to preserve a
Constitutional ideal. But that may not,
in fact, be entirely accurate. Despots,
autocrats and tyrants everywhere use
constitutionalism precisely to legitimize
their power. They claim unswerving
fidelity to the Constitution even as they
go about subverting it, either with way-
ward interpretations or—in ways both
invidious and insidious—by amending

uncomfortable Constitutional mandates. Any or all the methods and devices I outlined in my lecture are usually directed to exactly this end: to lay claim to continued constitutionalism while eviscerating the essentials. This leaves the nation-state with a pretence of a Constitution—a hollow shell.

To what then should one be expected to be committed?

I spoke about elections and choice. But what is the purpose of mandating elections every five years without an accompanying enforceable right to exercise that choice, that is to say, a right to vote, one that is at least a Constitutional right? This is still the subject of much debate among students and scholars of law.[17]

Gopnik's assertion therefore makes a demand of every citizen in a functioning Constitutional democracy: to commit ourselves to the essential Constitutional ideal—debate, plurality, dissent, informed choice at every stage—and to strive ceaselessly to prevent its undermining.

Two days after Constitution Day, on 28 November 2021, there appeared a remarkable communication. An open letter to 'fellow citizens', it had 102 signatories. Every one of them has held a significant post or position in the civil, foreign and police services with the central government and various state governments. As one, and with one voice, all 102 signatories condemned the concerted—and now flagrant—assault on 'civil society' and the 'new frontiers of war'. They wrote:

> Instead of exhorting the IPS probationers to abide by the values enshrined in the Constitution to which they had sworn allegiance, the NSA stressed the primacy of the representatives of the people, and the laws framed by them.
> [. . .]
> The NSA's clarion call for an onslaught on a demonised civil society is of a piece with

the narrative of hate targeting
defenders of Constitutional
values and human rights
that is regularly purveyed by
the high and mighty in the
establishment.[18]

There is hope yet.

One reaction to the lecture must be addressed. It was voiced by many who had heard my talk or read its text. To say that the internet, as a medium of expression, provides a bastion against attempts to stifle dissent is, my critics said, over-simplistic. It romanticizes the perils of the internet. Many pointed to specific cases of internet or online surveillance, fake news, social media manipulation and so on. I understood the argument to suggest that the internet cannot be a sufficiently strong bulwark.

First, the argument rather misses the point I was making. Governments everywhere find themselves unable to stop the tide of dissent *as once they could*. Even in our lifetimes, we had repressive governments that successfully thwarted and muzzled dissent. A vivid illustration is the push-back against Putin from within Russia. There have always been dissidents, and their dissents have come at great cost. But in the past, governments have been able to prevent those dissenting voices from being heard at all. It is not the existence of dissent but the silencing of it that is critical. In the days before the internet, that silencing was more easily achieved: pervasive state control of media, for instance. With the internet, this is simply impossible.

The internet is leaky. The internet is meant to be leaky. That is in its fundamental design, its technological DNA. On the internet, *things fall apart, the centre cannot hold*—because there *is* no centre. That is the quietly devastating strength of the internet. Dissents will, therefore, leak; they will slip out. Witness the Panama Papers, or Pegasus or virtually any form of disclosure that we have recently seen. A fraction of it may have been possible in the days before the internet, but the gathering of information and data on so vast a scale, with such penetration and accuracy, has been possible *only* because of internet technologies. With its distributed networks and layered linkages, the internet is, for a repressive government, very much like the cup of Tantalus, always just out of reach. Trying to stop bits and pieces of it is like trying to catch a piece of a cloud—and that particular metaphor could not be more appropriate. The *only* way to stop this digital leakiness is to shut it down entirely. But that is like burning down your house with you inside it, because government functioning comes to an almost total halt without connectivity. Without the internet, what will a government do? Revert to smoke signals, drumbeats and fleet-of-foot messengers with papyrus scrolls?

The criticism also rests on some incorrect assumptions. The fact that the internet is abused by governments in some fashion or other—huge data gathering, deep surveillance, manipulation of media—does not mean that the *whole* of the internet is perverted to these uses, nor that the free parts of it have been totally obliterated. Indeed, the resistance to surveillance and the fight against data gathering, and the ascendance of newly articulated rights ('the right to be left alone'; 'the right to be forgotten') are all made possible because of the internet,

not despite it. The right to privacy
was earlier denied recognition as a
Constitutional right. It is now firmly
entrenched as part of the right to *life* in
Indian jurisprudence. The recent expan-
sions of the right to privacy are more
sophisticated and subtle. The 'right to be
left alone' does not mean the right to stay
off the internet, but the right to use the
internet and *yet* be left alone. Similarly,
the right to be forgotten has critically
important implications. Consider this:
a juvenile is in conflict with the law.
There is a digital record of this conflict, a
'criminal record'. Perhaps the offence is
slight. Perhaps there is an acquittal. Or
perhaps the person serves out the law's

sentencing. In adulthood, in *any* of these three scenarios, 'the right to be forgotten' means the right to have one's digital footprint erased from publicly accessible databases so that one's future, both online and in the real world, is not forever clouded by the past. This is a classic example of digital power over an individual, and the individual's rights emerging triumphant. The assumption, therefore, that the government should not have any role or presence for the internet to be a tool against oppression is false.

The second incorrect assumption is about the nature of the internet itself. The internet is not nice. It is not meant to be nice. It is not meant to be anything.

The criticism fails because it hinges on this assumption, that the internet is a nice, even playing field with rules of fair play and decency. I argue that precisely because it is none of those things that the internet is so feared by governments everywhere.

I stand by my argument in the lecture. I reject the notion and the argument that the abuse of the internet, or of some of its possibilities, by governments weakens or threatens the internet's power to be a medium of free expression. One thing appears to me to be plain—at the core of the internet, whether by design or accident, there lies one concept: liberty of the individual.

NOTES

1   Ian McDonald, *River of Gods* (London: Simon and Schuster, 2004).

2   Madhav Khosla, *India's Founding Moment* (Cambridge, MA: Harvard University Press, 2020).

3   Rohit De, *A People's Constitution: The Everyday Life of Law in the Indian Republic* (Princeton, NJ: Princeton University Press), p. 5.

4   De, *A People's Constitution*, p. 9.

5   See, for instance, three articles by A. G. Noorani in *Frontline*: 'The Plague of Sedition', 13 March 2020, available at: https://tinyurl.com/ycd2gxv4; 'Colonial

Relic', 15 April 2016, available at:
https://tinyurl.com/yhasnxpr; 'How a
Supreme Court Judgment Brought Back the
Sedition Law in India', 15 January 2021,
available at: https://tinyurl.com/yhhv42xr.
All weblinks last accessed on 8 April 2022.

6 See, among others, the following by
Abhinav Chandrachud: *Republic of Rhetoric:
Free Speech and the Constitution of India*
(New Delhi: India Viking, 2017); 'Freedom
from Sedition', *The Hindu*, 15 August 2021,
available at: https://tinyurl.com/y6v8cc54;
'Plague of 1896 Redefined Sedition.
Coronavirus Mustn't Bring in Laws That
Outlive Crisis', *The Print*, 24 March 2020,
available at: https://theprint.in/?p=386552.
Both weblinks last accessed on 8 April 2022.

7 Manan Ahmed Asif, *The Loss of Hindustan:
The Invention of India* (Cambridge, MA:
Harvard University Press, 2020).

8 Romila Thapar, *Voices of Dissent: An Essay* (London: Seagull Books, 2020).

9 Anne Applebaum, 'The Bad Guys Are Winning', *The Atlantic*, 15 November 2021, available at: https://bit.ly/3NHgVVh (last accessed on 30 March 2022).

10 Adam Zamoyski, *Phantom Terror: The Threat of Revolution and the Repression of Liberty, 1789–1848* (New York: Basic Books, 2015).

11 Jacket text of Zamoyski, *Phantom Terror*.

12 Jonathan Rauch, *Kindly Inquisitors* (Chicago: University of Chicago Press, 2014), pp. 127–28.

13 Learned Hand, *The Spirit of Liberty: Papers and Addresses of Learned Hand* (New York: Knopf, 1952).

14 Pratap Bhanu Mehta, 'The Indian Supreme Court and the Art of Democratic

Positioning' in Mark Tushnet and Madhav Khosla (eds), *Unstable Constitutionalism: Law and Politics in South Asia* (New York: Cambridge University Press, 2015), pp. 233–60; here, p. 234.

15 *Romesh Thappar v. The State of Madras*, 26 May 1950 (AIR 1950 SC 124, 1950 SCR 594).

16 Adam Gopnik, 'Kurt Gödel's Loophole and Donald Trump's Defiance', *The New Yorker* (26 November 2021), available at: https://bit.ly/3iWC5R6 (last accessed on 30 March 2022).

17 See, for instance: Rajeev Kadambi, 'Right to Vote as a Fundamental Right: Mistaking the Woods for Trees, *PUCL v Union of India*', *Indian Journal of Constitutional Law* 3 (April 2009): 181–94, available at: https://bit.ly/3LCwP1l (last accessed on 30

March 2022); Saurabh Bhattacharjee, 'The "Fundamentals" of the Right to Vote and its Constitutional Status', *NALSAR Student Law Review* 1(39) (2005): 39–50.

18 Various authors, 'Civil Society: Enemy of the State?' Available at: https://bit.ly/3tYLnlP (last accessed on 1 April 2022).